W9-CDX-519

THE STORY OF

Model T Fords

by David K. Wright

Gareth Stevens Publishing
A WORLD ALMANAC EDUCATION GROUP COMPANY

Please visit our web site at: www.garethstevens.com
For a free color catalog describing Gareth Stevens Publishing's
list of high-quality books and multimedia programs,
call 1-800-542-2595 (USA) or 1-800-387-3178 (Canada).
Gareth Stevens Publishing's fax: (414) 332-3567.

Library of Congress Cataloging-in-Publication Data

Wright, David K.
    The story of Model T Fords / by David K. Wright.
        p. cm. — (Classic cars: an imagination library series)
    Includes bibliographical references and index.
    Summary: Surveys the history of the Model T, one of the earliest
and most popular cars in America.
        ISBN 0-8368-3192-6 (lib. bdg.)
        1. Ford Model T Automobile—History—Juvenile literature.
    [1. Ford Model T Automobile—History.] I. Title.
    TL215.F37W75   2002
    629.222'2—dc21   2002021181

First published in 2002 by
Gareth Stevens Publishing
A World Almanac Education Group Company
330 West Olive Street, Suite 100
Milwaukee, WI 53212 USA

Text: David K. Wright
Cover design and page layout: Scott M. Krall
Series editor: Jim Mezzanotte
Picture Researcher: Diane Laska-Swanke

Photo credits: Cover, pp. 5, 11, 13, 21 © Ron Kimball; p. 7, Neg. #833.198, From the Collections
of Henry Ford Museum & Greenfield Village; p. 9 Photofest; p. 15, Neg. #O.1262, From the
Collections of Henry Ford Museum & Greenfield Village; p. 17, Neg. #O.716, From the Collections
of Henry Ford Museum & Greenfield Village; p. 19 Courtesy of the Detroit Public Library, National
Automotive History Collection

Printed in the United States of America

1 2 3 4 5 6 7 8 9 06 05 04 03 02

Front cover: **Henry Ford's Model T proved
that cars were here to stay. This 1915
Model T is an early convertible!**

TABLE OF CONTENTS

Words that appear in the glossary are printed in **boldface** type the first time they occur in the text.

THE FIRST MODEL T

Henry Ford grew up on a farm in Michigan. He learned about mechanical things by working on farm machinery. As an adult, he **designed** and built some of the first cars ever made in the United States. One of his most famous creations is the Model T.

Henry Ford's factory began making the Model T in 1908. The car had many wooden parts. It does not look very sturdy, especially compared to modern cars. But in its day, it was one of the most reliable cars on the road.

Many of the features that are found on modern cars began with the Model T. The Model T, for example, had its steering wheel on the left side. Other carmakers soon copied this feature.

Model T Fords were good, reliable cars, but they look different from the cars of today. This 1915 Model T has wooden wheels and no side windows!

MAKING THE MODEL T

Before long, everyone wanted to own a Model T. No matter how fast the Ford Motor Company built its cars, orders piled up.

The company began putting cars together on an **assembly line**. As the **chassis** of a Model T moved through the factory, workers attached parts to it. By 1914, a Model T chassis could be produced in less than two hours!

Henry Ford realized that his workers could also be his customers if they could afford to buy his cars. He doubled the pay of his assembly-line workers and kept the price of the Model T low.

These workers are attaching an engine to a Model T chassis. They may have driven home in Model Ts they built themselves!

THE MOVIE STAR CAR

Model T Fords seemed to be everywhere, including the movies. Comedians in silent films performed hair-raising stunts in the cars. Around the world, the Model T Ford was the first car that many people saw, often on a movie screen. People even gave the car nicknames. They called it a "Tin Lizzy" or a "flivver."

The **engineers** at the Ford Motor Company kept finding ways to make the Model T for less money. After 1914, for example, the company began offering the car only in black to save money on buying many different kinds of paint! The company also replaced the wooden steering wheel in the Model T with one made of a special plastic called Fordite.

In early silent films, Fords could often be seen carrying funny people around. These fellows were known as the "Keystone Kops."

A BESTSELLER

The Model T became popular for several reasons. It sold for as little as $360, so many people could afford it. The car was also reliable, always getting people where they wanted to go. The Model T was not a very fast car, but for most people, it still had plenty of "pep," or power.

Model T Fords came in many shapes and sizes. People could buy a sporty two-seater or a larger, four-door sedan. Model T Fords were **modified** so they could be used for different jobs. They became ambulances, delivery trucks, school buses, and other special vehicles.

This 1914 Model T Ford is a two-seat speedster, an early kind of sports car. It was made before Model T Fords only came in black.

HARD AT WORK

The Model T changed the way people lived and worked. With the Model T, people and things could get around quickly. People used Model T Fords to deliver groceries, **haul** furniture, even save lives. Model T Fords helped everyone, from farmers to the police.

The Ford Motor Company kept finding ways to improve the Model T so the car became even more useful to people. In 1915, for example, the company replaced the Model T's weak oil lamps with much brighter electric headlights. Now people could travel more easily at night.

People used Model T Fords for all kinds of jobs. A farmer used this 1914 Model T delivery truck to sell fruits and vegetables.

ON THE MOVE

The greatest year for the Model T was 1923. That year, more than two million Model T Fords were sold. By then, many people were using the Model T to take long trips. People who had never left their hometowns were now getting out to do some sightseeing!

With so many people on the move, new roads were needed. Engineers began making plans for new roads and highway systems. People also began living in neighborhoods that were farther away from the centers of cities and towns.

With the Model T Ford, people could really get around — and so could animals! This Model T was modified so it could carry a goat.

TEN MILLION SOLD!

By 1924, the total number of Model T Fords sold had reached more than ten million! In many parts of the world, the Model T Ford and other cars had replaced horses as the main form of **transportation**.

Model T Fords were being used by all kinds of people for all kinds of jobs. People built trucks, vans, and even tractors on the Model T chassis. The Model T Ford helped make Detroit, Michigan, the worldwide center of the automobile industry.

These Model T Fords were built in a single day at the factory! By the 1920s, there were millions of Model T Fords all over the world.

THE LAST MODEL T

By 1926, the Model T had become **outdated**. The Ford Motor Company had made many improvements to the car and now offered it in different colors, such as maroon, green, and grey. But other car companies were selling more cars.

Chevrolet was Ford's biggest **rival**. The cars made by Chevrolet were faster and more powerful than the Model T. The Ford Motor Company designed a new car, called the Model A. In 1927, the company stopped making the Model T and started making the Model A. The Model T had reached the end of the line.

Here are three early Fords. The car on the right is a Model K, built in 1906. The car in the middle is a 1908 Model T. A 1928 Model A is on the left.

THE IMPORTANCE OF THE MODEL T

The Model T might not have been the fastest or fanciest car, but it allowed people to travel as they never had before. The car **influenced** the way people worked and played — and even where they decided to build their homes.

Henry Ford's Model T proved that the automobile was for everyone and that it was here to stay. The Ford Motor Company built and sold a total of fifteen million Model T Fords. The huge popularity of the Model T changed life in the United States and other parts of the world.

A Model T such as this one might look old-fashioned, but Model T Fords helped change the world in the twentieth century!

MORE TO READ AND VIEW

Books (Nonfiction)   *All Aboard Cars.* Catherine Daly-Weir (Grosset & Dunlap)
Henry Ford. Inventors and Creators (series). Sheila Wyborn
  (Kidhaven)
Henry Ford. Trailblazers of the Modern World (series). Michael Burgan.
  (World Almanac Library)
Henry Ford: An Unauthorized Biography. Heinemann Profiles (series).
  John Malam (Heinemann Library)
Henry Ford: Building Cars for Everyone. Historical American Biographies
  (series). Pat McCarthy (Enslow Publishers)
Model T: How Henry Ford Built a Legend. David Weitzman
  (Crown Publishing)

Videos (Nonfiction)   *A&E Top 10: Cars That Changed the Automobile Industry.* (A&E)
Classic Cars with Edward Hermann. (A&E)
Henry Ford: Tin Lizzy Tycoon. (A&E)
Inventors of the World: Henry Ford. (Schlessinger Media)
Ten Greatest American Cars. (A&E)

PLACES TO WRITE AND VISIT

Here are three places to contact for more information:

Auto World Car Museum
Business Route 54
Fulton, MO 65251
USA
1-573-642-2080

**Henry Ford Museum
& Greenfield Village**
20900 Oakwood Blvd.
Dearborn, MI 48124
USA
1-313-271-1620
www.hfmgv.org

National Automobile Museum
10 Lake Street South
Reno, NV 89501
USA
1-775-333-9300
**www.automuseum.org/
info.html**

WEB SITES

Web sites change frequently, but we believe the following web sites are going to last. You can also use good search engines, such as **Yahooligans!** [**www.yahooligans.com**] or **Google** [**www.google.com**], to find more information about Model T Fords. Here are some keywords to help you: *assembly line, Ford Motor Company, Henry Ford, Model A, Model T,* and *quadricycle.*

clubs.hemmings.com/mtfctulsa/ ourcars.htm
This site shows pictures of Model T Fords from the *Model T Ford Club of Tulsa.*

www.hfmgv.org/education/smartfun/ welcome.html
Model T Road Trip is an interactive site from the *Henry Ford Museum & Greenfield Village* web site. Follow a fictional family as they take a trip across the United States in 1919!

www.hfmgv.org/exhibits/showroom/ 1908/model.t.html
This site is also from the *Henry Ford Museum & Greenfield Village* web site. It has photos and interesting facts about the Model T and other antique cars.

www.modelt.org
This is the web site for the *Model T Ford Club International.* It has a lot of neat information and photos, and it also has a list of how the Model T changed from one year to the next.

www.mtfca.com
This is the web site for the *Model T Ford Club of America.* It has a photo gallery with pictures of a Model T from every year of production.

www.t-ford.co.uk/pic.htm
This photo gallery is from the *Model T Ford Register of Great Britain.* It has many old pictures of Model T Fords.

GLOSSARY

You can find these words on the pages listed. Reading a word in a sentence helps you understand it even better.

assembly line (uh-SEM-blee line) — a system that makes things by moving them through a factory while workers attach parts 6

chassis (CHASS-ee) — a frame that holds the body and the engine of a car 6, 16

designed (de-ZINED) — created the plans needed to build something 4, 18

engineers (ehn-jin-EARZ) — people who plan the construction of buildings or machines 8, 14

haul (HAWL) — to carry something in a car, truck, or other vehicle 12

influenced (IN-flew-enst) — had an effect on something 20

modified (MOD-if-eyed) — changed from the original 10, 14

outdated (owt-DATE-id) — no longer modern or up-to-date 18

rival (RY-vul) — a person or group that competes with another person or group 18

transportation (tranz-poor-TAY-shun) — the method or equipment people use to travel from one place to another 16

INDEX